The Honey Bees Truth Be Told

Written and Illustrated by Paul J. Giordano

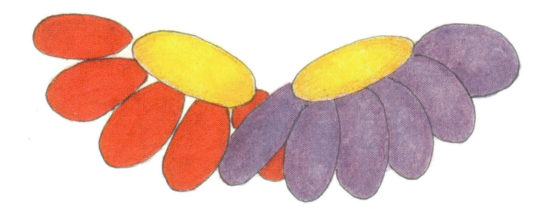

Copyright © 2012 by Paula J. Giordano

The Honey Bees Truth Be Told
by Paula J. Giordano

Printed in the United States of America

ISBN 9781624193545

All rights reserved solely by the author. The author guarantees all contents are original and do not infringe upon the legal rights of any other person or work. No part of this book may be reproduced in any form without the permission of the author. The views expressed in this book are not necessarily those of the publisher.

Unless otherwise indicated, Bible quotations are taken from The Holy Bible, New International Version. Copyright © 1973, 1978, 1984 by International Bible Society, Zondervan Publishing House.

www.xulonpress.com

Dedication

This book is dedicated to Christopher, Veronica and Joshua. My three beautiful children, God has graciously given to me. Each so different, true individuals, collectively bringing me more joy than a mother could ever imagine.

I fell in love with each of you from the moment I held you in my arms, and that love continues to grow as each year flies by. My prayer for all of you is; that you love Jesus with all your heart, make Him the Lord of your life and never depart from Him.

Acknowledgement

I want to thank the Holy Spirit for entrusting me with the dream of the Honey Bees and the soon to be Rolling Soup Kitchen. I also want to acknowledge my son Christopher who has walked alongside me through this journey. I could never have had my books published without his knowledge of technology, and his ability to take my words and illustrations and put them into digital files to present to my publisher. I am so thankful for his wonderful ability to think creatively, and outside the box in the world of marketing. God has blessed you with many gifts, thank you my boy.

In addition there have been many others I would like to mention that have also been instrumental in assisting me to realize my dream they are, my niece Dana Arace, and my youngest son Joshua Alicea who edited book one. My dear friends Rhonda Calandrillo who assisted in book one. Donna Miller and her son Michael Miller who edited book two. May God bless all of you for your love and support.

Mrs. Pea and Bella were invited to Shannon's house for a play date. Bella and her mommy were flying to Shannon's house, and stopped in the Flower Patch. Mrs. Pea reminded Bella, "We are about to pass through the Black Raven Forest. We need to concentrate and hold our buzzers silent. If we don't, those Bad Boys will surely try to catch us and make us their lunch." "Ok Mommy, I will try to keep my buzzer quiet," Bella replied.

The bees saw all the ravens resting on the tree limbs. "Oh, it is so hard to keep my buzzer quiet," Bella thought. Suddenly she couldn't hold her buzzer anymore, and she heard the familiar sound. BZZZZZZZZZZZZZZZ!!!

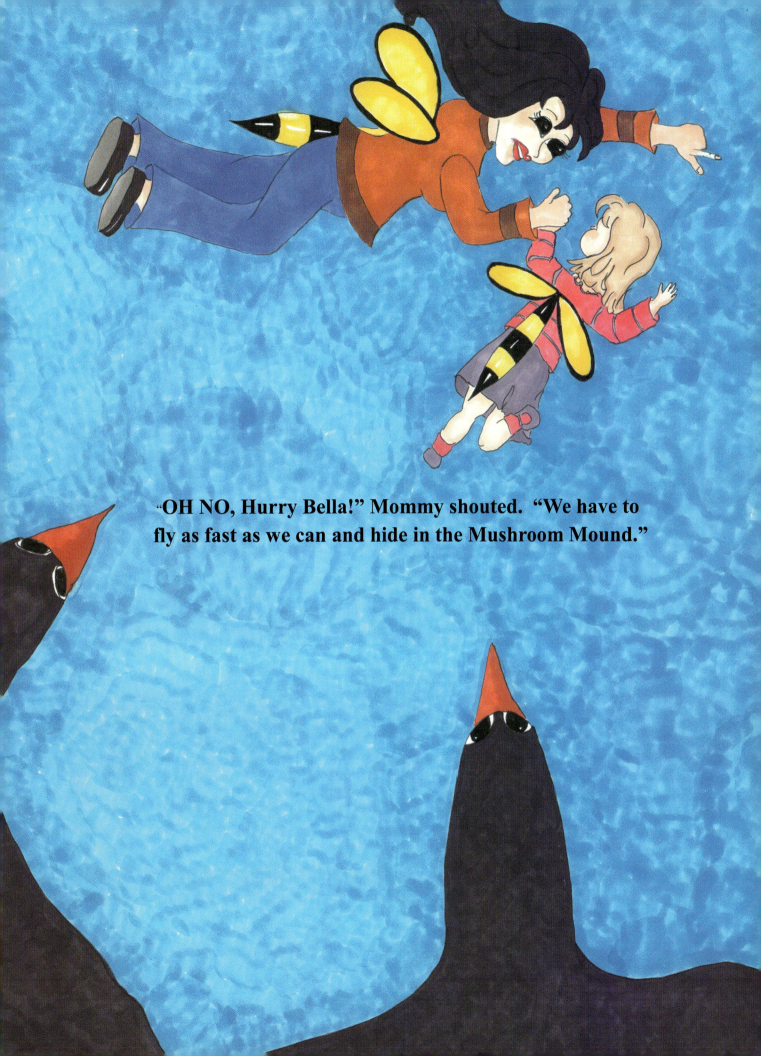

"OH NO, Hurry Bella!" Mommy shouted. "We have to fly as fast as we can and hide in the Mushroom Mound."

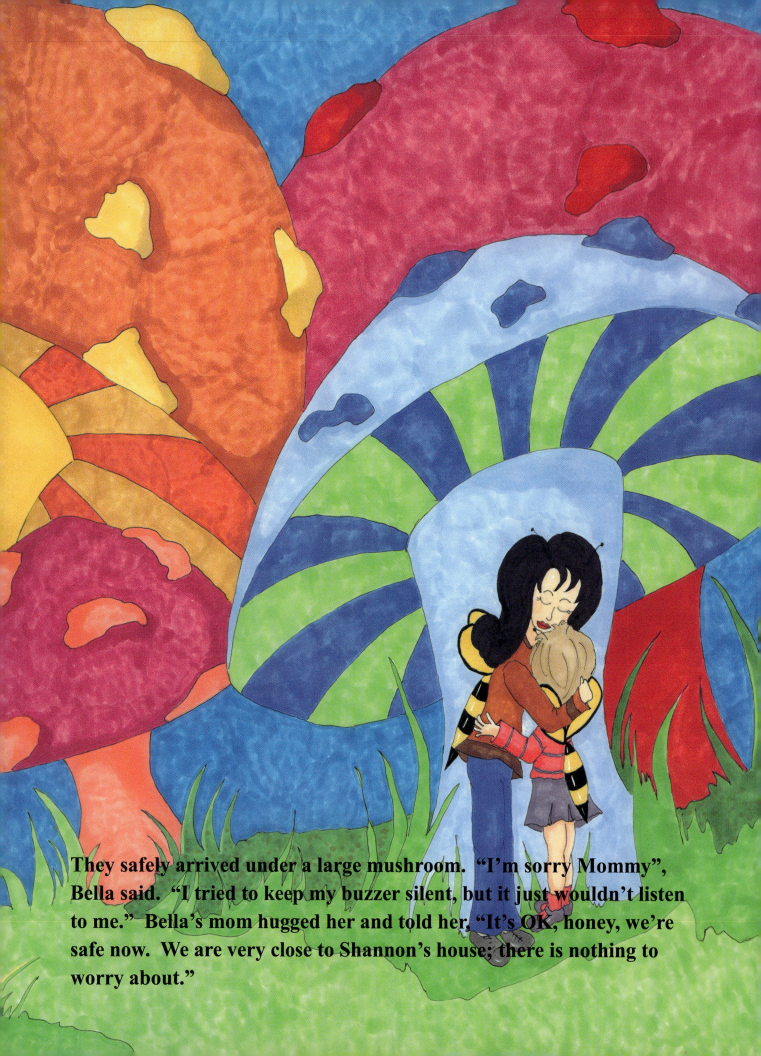

They safely arrived under a large mushroom. "I'm sorry Mommy", Bella said. "I tried to keep my buzzer silent, but it just wouldn't listen to me." Bella's mom hugged her and told her, "It's OK, honey, we're safe now. We are very close to Shannon's house; there is nothing to worry about."

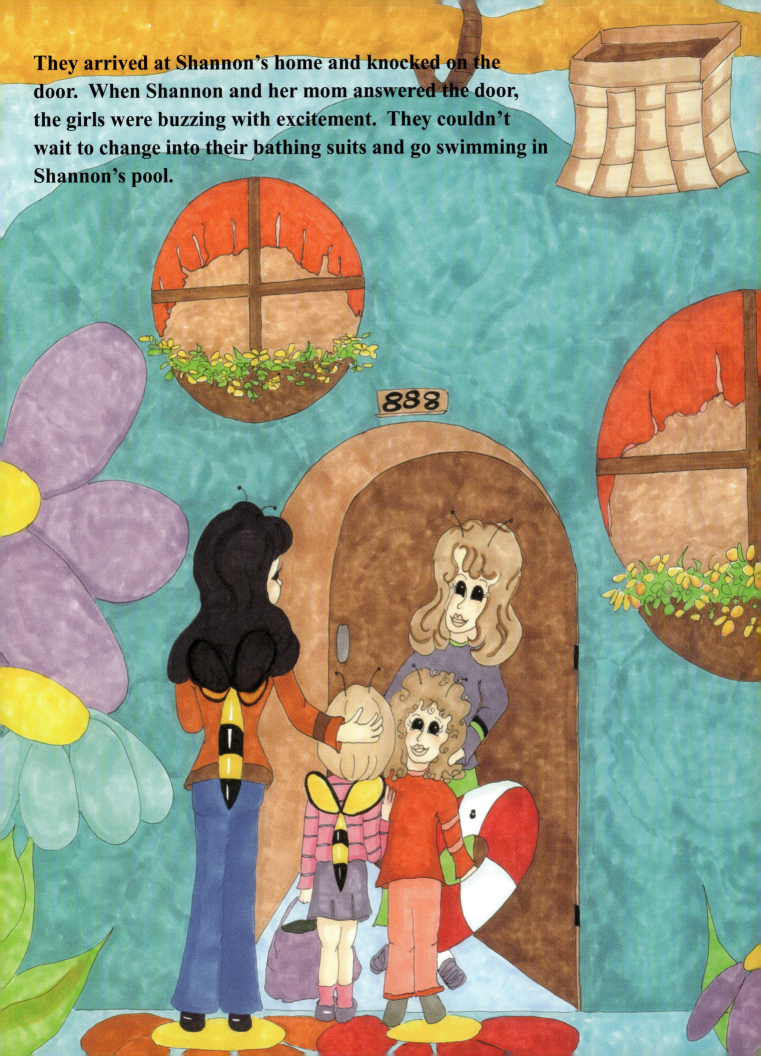

They arrived at Shannon's home and knocked on the door. When Shannon and her mom answered the door, the girls were buzzing with excitement. They couldn't wait to change into their bathing suits and go swimming in Shannon's pool.

While the two moms were talking, the bees were having lots of fun playing water tag, and diving for colored stones. They were floating in their tubes, when Shannon started talking about her family's trip to the Beetle Bash Amusement Park. Shannon described the Crazy Caterpillar, "It was so high, I thought my belly was going to leave my body," she said. "Oh, I know that coaster you're talking about," Bella said "I love it! It was so much fun; my belly does flip flops."

Mrs. Kiddle, Shannon's mom, brought the girls some snacks and the new arrival, their friend Rosie. Mrs. Kiddle overheard the girls talking about the amusement park. She commented, "Oh Bella, I didn't know you and your family also went to the amusement park." Shannon jumped in and answered for Bella, "Yes Mom, and Bella went on the Crazy Caterpillar too, and she wasn't at all afraid." Rosie added, "NO WAY, BELLA! That coaster was too scary for me; I wouldn't even go on it!" "Oh it was no big thing," Bella said. Mrs. Pea heard the whole conversation. She was upset and sad because she knew Bella wasn't telling the truth to her friends and Mrs. Kiddle. She decided she would speak to Bella when they got home.

When Bella and Mrs. Pea arrived at home, Mrs. Pea sadly told Bella, "I heard you talking to Shannon. Why would you tell her you went to the park when it's not true?" Bella replied, "Well, if we had gone to that park you know I wouldn't have been afraid to go on that coaster. I go on all the big roller coasters, and I love them!" Her mom responded, "That's true Bella, but telling Shannon you went to that park and on that coaster was a lie. You don't have to make up stories to impress a friend; being truthful is more important. " "When someone tells a lie they usually get caught. One lie always leads to another but eventually the truth comes out. And when it does, you will not be trusted, and with good reason. I'm going to have to punish you my girl. No playing on the bubble tube for a week! Please think about what we talked about, okay?"

A few days later, Bella was having another play date with her friend Shannon. Shannon continued talking about her day at the amusement park. She was remembering how scared she was while on the Crazy Caterpillar. Mrs. Pea was nearby making the girls some lunch. She heard the bees talking. Mrs. Pea was waiting for Bella's response to Shannon talking about the roller coaster.

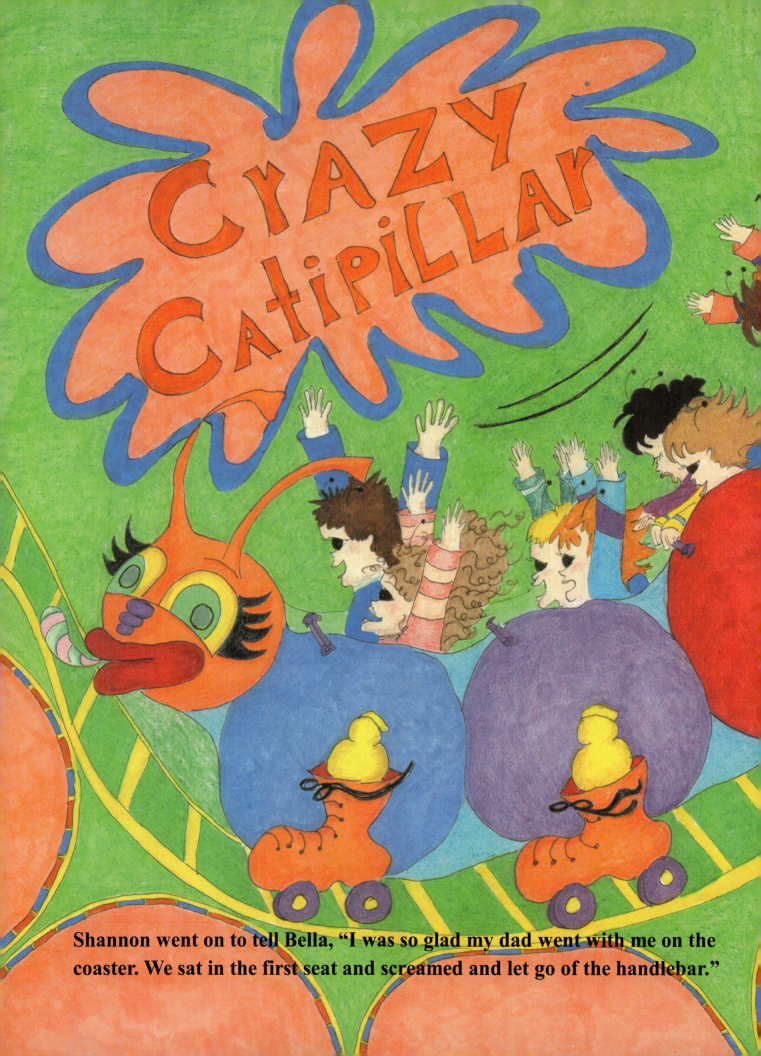

Shannon went on to tell Bella, "I was so glad my dad went with me on the coaster. We sat in the first seat and screamed and let go of the handlebar."

"Wasn't the park so much fun Bella?" she continued, "Did you love the clowns, and the bees walking on stilts? Did you go on the other rides and play games too?" Bella answered, "Oh yes, I loved the entire park and can't wait to go back again." Suddenly Bella remembered what her mom said, "One lie will surely lead to another." Her mom was right. Mrs. Pea heard Bella lie again, and was very upset.

Shannon and her mom were on their way home when Mrs. Pea asked to speak to Bella. "I heard you speaking to Shannon again…" Before her mom could finish, Bella jumped in, "I know Mommy. I am so sorry, as soon as the words came out of my mouth I realized I was doing it again." Mrs. Pea continued, "You could have admitted you told a lie, instead of adding more lies to your story. We need to pray and ask Jesus to help you with this."

They both bowed their heads in prayer. "Dear Jesus, please help my Bella. Help her to know first how precious she is to you. Just like it says in your word, that she is fearfully and wonderfully made by you Father. Let her know you love her just the way she is Lord, that she doesn't have to tell lies to impress people. Help her to be more like you, Jesus, honest and true. Amen.

A few weeks later, the Honey Bees met some friends at Twinkle Park. Jakub, Bella, NiNi and Rosie were sliding down the huge elephant leaf slides, squealing in delight! Their friends, Ming and Jose, also joined them, and added to the joyous shouts and screams. While Jakub pushed Rosie on the swing, all the other children sat down and started talking. Bella was spouting about how she could do all these really hard moves on the balance beam. "Bella!" Jakub scolded. "You cannot, and stop telling stories!" "There she goes again," Jakub thought. "She's always telling lies."

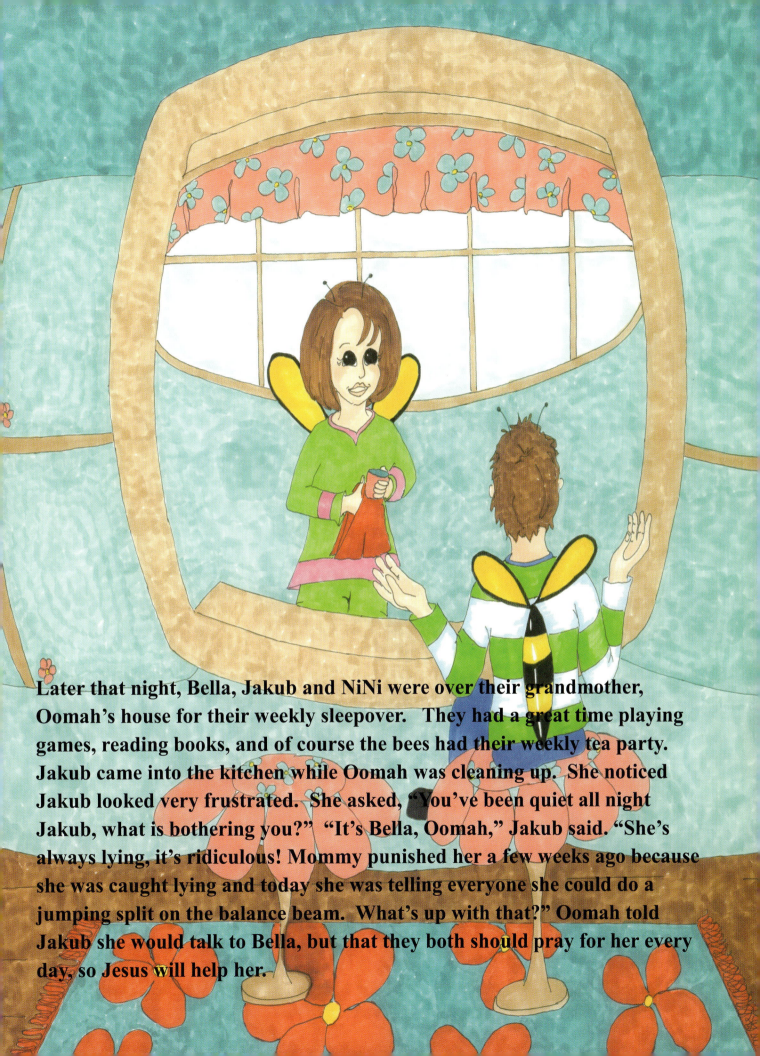

Later that night, Bella, Jakub and NiNi were over their grandmother, Oomah's house for their weekly sleepover. They had a great time playing games, reading books, and of course the bees had their weekly tea party. Jakub came into the kitchen while Oomah was cleaning up. She noticed Jakub looked very frustrated. She asked, "You've been quiet all night Jakub, what is bothering you?" "It's Bella, Oomah," Jakub said. "She's always lying, it's ridiculous! Mommy punished her a few weeks ago because she was caught lying and today she was telling everyone she could do a jumping split on the balance beam. What's up with that?" Oomah told Jakub she would talk to Bella, but that they both should pray for her every day, so Jesus will help her.

While Oomah was cuddling with Bella, she asked her, "I heard you were recently punished for being dishonest." "Yes, Oomah," Bella sadly replied, "and Mommy told me once I told one lie more would follow, and she was right!" Bella's eyes filled with tears. Oomah hugged her. "It's going to be OK my girl. We are going to ask Jesus to help you. But first you need to remember that you were made by the Creator of the Universe. He doesn't make mistakes. He has given you wonderful gifts and made you unique and special. So you don't have to pretend you can do certain things to impress people. Now let's see what Jesus says about lying in the Bible."

Oomah got her Bible and found Proverbs 6: 16-17. This is what it says Bella, "There are six things the Lord hates, seven that are detestable to him: haughty eyes, a lying tongue…" "Ugh!" Bella gasped. "I know you didn't realize how strongly God felt about lying, my love, and lets read more," Oomah added. "In Proverbs 12:22, the word of God says" "The Lord detests lying lips…" Bella's eyes widened. Oomah added, "Jesus hates sin, and lying is a sin. Jesus is truth; we can always depend on Him and everything He says in the Bible because He always tells the truth, He never lies. Jesus describes the devil as being "the father of lies." I know you love Jesus and want to be like Him, and not like the Devil.

"How am I going to fix this, Oomah?" Bella asked. The first thing Oomah told her was that she needed to ask Jesus to forgive her for all the lies. "But what if He is angry at me?" Bella inquired. Oomah reminded Bella that Jesus loves us so much; I know He will absolutely forgive you, that is why He went to the cross for us, so we can have our sins forgiven. "Ok let's do that right now Oomah." Bella said as she got on her knees to pray. Bella asked Jesus to forgive her for all the lies. Then she asked Jesus to help her remember how important it is to tell the truth, and to be honest from now on.

After they prayed, Oomah tucked Bella into bed. "Bella you should be honest with your friends too. Tell them you can't do jumping splits and that you never went to the Beetle Bash Amusement Park." Oomah also suggested Bella should ask them to forgive her for all the lies. Bella didn't want to lie anymore so she promised Oomah she would do just that.

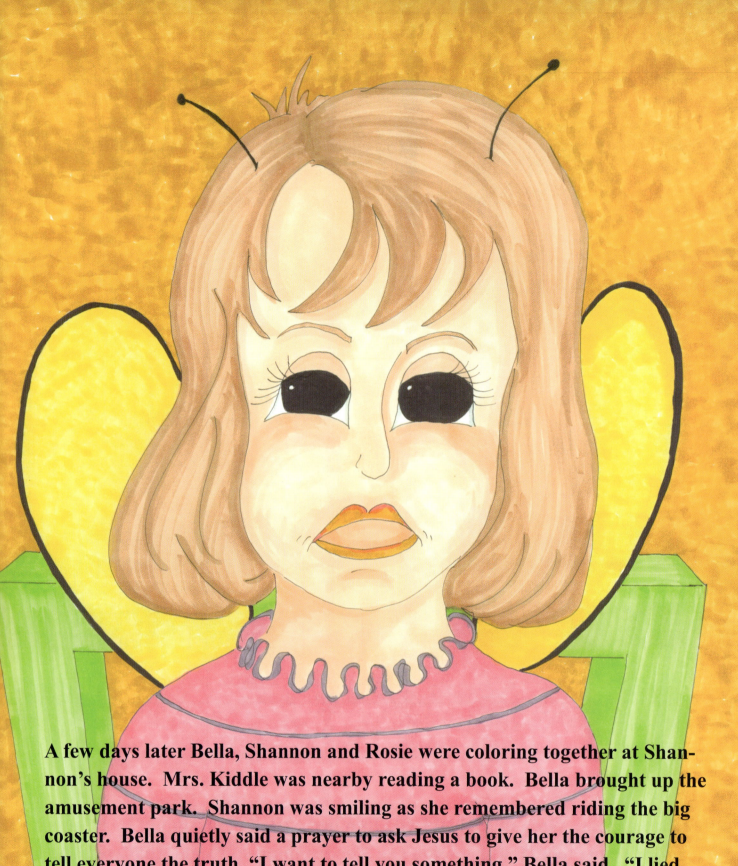

A few days later Bella, Shannon and Rosie were coloring together at Shannon's house. Mrs. Kiddle was nearby reading a book. Bella brought up the amusement park. Shannon was smiling as she remembered riding the big coaster. Bella quietly said a prayer to ask Jesus to give her the courage to tell everyone the truth. "I want to tell you something," Bella said. "I lied when I told you I went to the Beetle Bash Amusement Park and rode the Crazy Caterpillar; I have never been there. And I can't do a flying split on the balance beam either. I am really sorry; I hope you are not angry and can forgive me."

Shannon smiled, "Bella, I'm not mad. I know you love coasters and go on lots of big rides that I would be too scared to go on. So I don't know why you lied, but it's OK, Bella." Rosie admitted she couldn't do any tricks on the balance beam either, so it was no big thing. Mrs. Kiddle told Bella she was very proud of her for being brave enough to tell the truth and ask for forgiveness.

The next day, NiNi's Mom brought Jakub, Bella and NiNi to meet their friends for ice cream. The bees were all chattering away as they devoured their ice cream cones. Ming was talking about her latest gymnastics class. Bella was just about to jump in and talk about her flying split on the balance beam, but she stopped and remembered that verse in the Bible that said "The Lord detests lying lips." "Thank you Jesus for reminding me," she said to herself, and remained quiet.

As the children were heading home, Shannon told everyone she and her family were returning to the Beetle Bash Amusement Park on Saturday. She was all excited because she was going to ride the Crazy Caterpillar again. Bella was just about to chime in that she wasn't afraid to ride that coaster and remembered the Bible verse Oomah showed her which said "God hates a lying tongue." She also remembered that God loves her just the way she is, that He made her unique and special, so she doesn't have to make up stories to impress her friends. "I love you too, Jesus, she thought. Thank you Jesus." The End.

So my Bees, do you ever have a hard time telling the truth? We all make mistakes sometimes, but I am very grateful that when I do mess up, I can ask Jesus to forgive me. How about you? When you invite Jesus into your heart, you can go to Him when you make mistakes too and ask Him for forgiveness. If you are truly sorry for what you did, He will forgive you and help you to become more like Him.

All you have to do is ask Him, like this: Dear Jesus, I know you are the son of God. Thank you for dying on the cross for me. Please come into my heart. Forgive me for all the mistakes I have made, and help me to be more like you. I love you Jesus. Amen.

Jesus loves you so much! He has also made YOU unique and special. Make Him a part of each day by reading your Bible and talking to Him regularly. I hope you and your family will find a good Bible teaching church so you can learn all about God's amazing love and His plan for your life!

See you next time my Bees!

About The Author

Paula J. Giordano

Born in Brooklyn New York. Raised and currently living in New Jersey. Serving the Lord for twenty years at Calvary Temple of Wayne. The series and illustrations are Holy Ghost birthed and inspired. The Honey Bees series has three goals:

To teach children a life lesson in each book. Finding the resolution to the lesson by having a relationship with Jesus Christ and reading the Bible, God's blueprint for life. At the end of each book the reader is given an opportunity to invite Jesus into their heart. To start and support a rolling soup kitchen through the Hope Ministry of Calvary Temple of Wayne, by pledging half of all profits donated to the ministry.

Visit The Honey Bees at www.TheHoneyBeesBook.com